YEARS SPENT

EXPLORING POETRY IN ADVENTURE, LIFE AND LOVE

LALIT KUMAR

Notion Press Media Pvt Ltd

No. 50, Chettiyar Agaram Main Road,
Vanagaram, Chennai, Tamil Nadu – 600 095

First Published by Notion Press 2021
Copyright © Lalit Kumar 2021
All Rights Reserved.

ISBN 978-1-68494-626-6
International ISBN 979-8-88704-884-0

Dedication

To my family and friends

Contents

Epilogue   **133**

Acknowledgement

I would like to sincerely thank my family and friends who supported me as this book took shape. Some of them would often be kind enough to be my primary critics and provide their honest feedback. I would also like to thank the 'Poetry of Diaspora' group in the San Francisco Bay Area, a community of like-minded people to share and exchange ideas with.

Foreword

Poetry is omnipresent. When prose fails to speak to the human condition, poetry can fill the void with nuance. Pandemic poetry, written by Lalit Kumar, has resonated with the readers of the San Francisco Bay Area-based magazine *India Currents*. Now, he ventures into a new medium with his debut book of poems *Years Spent: Exploring Poetry in Adventure, Life and Love* which invites us into his life's journey. Sit on your comfiest couch, take a sip of hot *chai*, and dive into Kumar's intimate moments of hope, disappointment, success, failure, love, loss, and migration. In the process, we indulge in his passion for living life to its maximum potential. Poems like *Across the Border* and *Roots* are sure to pull in first and second-generation immigrants who are at a crossroads with their identity.

May we all embark on an adventurous journey with similar zeal to Kumar's. Happy Reading!

– Srishti Prabha,
Managing Editor of *India Currents*

"We read and write poetry because we are members of the human race. And the human race is filled with passion. And medicine, law, business, engineering are noble pursuits and necessary to sustain life. But poetry, beauty, romance, love, these are what we stay alive for..."

"That you are here - that life exists, and identity; that the powerful play goes on and you may contribute a verse. That the powerful play goes on and you may contribute a verse. What will your verse be?"

– Robin Williams _in Dead Poets Society_

Preface

I have often been asked what attracted me to poetry or how poetry found its way towards me. I could answer it by using clichés like 'poetry is just another creative outlet like painting or sculpting', but it sounded too pedantic to me. Instead, I choose to answer in a short verse as below -

When you have
too many ideas,
and too little time,
Scribble a sentence
Or type a few lines
on your notepad app,
And see the poetry in you
taking shape
word by word,
line by line.

Let it flow
for who knows,
you are bleeding verses
in the dull ramparts
of your charmed life.
Tomorrow,
someone might look back at you.

And who knows,
might discover
The true, 'You'.

In essence, poetry is something that needs to come out of you, unforced and unabated. A quote by Rudyard Kipling reflects the strength that poetry carries within itself: *"Words are, of course, the most powerful drug used by mankind."* I would like to add that if words are drugs, then poetry is that inebriated state when you are floating mid-way between reality and imagination.

To put it more succinctly, poetry is an exploration of inner emotions in tandem with the outer world as one navigates through his or her life journey. I hope this book that you are holding in your hand right now, gives you a few magical moments of reflection, inspiration or enjoyment.

This book is organized into 5 different sections; each of which is thematically arranged and emotionally vibrant...

- Life and Exploration
- Freedom and Adventure
- Pain and Loss
- Success and Achievement
- Love and Passion

These poems have been written through my college days and into work-life; they gathered further momentum especially over the last couple of years. Every one of us goes through the phases of life stages: school, college, work and eventually find ourselves on a quest for inner fulfillment. I went on a similar exploration (both literally and metaphorically) and most of these poems are snippets from that journey. I completed my education from top schools in India and eventually went to the USA where I have lived and worked for more than a decade now. I like to call both these countries home and you may find that some of my poems in this book have an undercurrent of longing for the birth country and reflection of a new immigrant's experience. What is life without longing for something!

I have been fascinated with adventure sports in the recent past. Apart from participating in Triathlons, I went on to do skydiving, rock climbing, mountaineering, ocean kayaking, scuba diving, skiing, motorcycle racing, horse riding and so on. These physical activities, coupled with learning new skills, have been rejuvenating for the soul to an extent that it has found utterances in this book especially in the first two sections. The two other sections related to love and pain /loss are based on the respective universal themes that are easy to identify with. In the section on success and achievement, I have wrestled with my definition for constructs of success, approaching it from multiple lenses. I am sure that these poems will strike a chord with you as you read them.

The pandemic period has forced most of us to introspect and that's when I found the calling for completing a book of poems. *Years Spent: Exploring Poetry in Adventure, Life and Love* is an apt title in that sense, as it has captured my accruing changes in the thought process over the years.

The objective of this book is to help you, the readers to re-connect with your emotions as you traverse your life journey and enrich it with new thoughts, ideas and inspirations.

Introduction

My Poetry

My poetry is -

a silent twinge
hidden beneath
the veneers of words.

A deep chasm,
trailing along
the edges of time.

A burning desire
to seek
in thoughtless verses.

A mournful serenade,
poignant with
warm thoughts.

A full-blown passion
pining for
ardent love.

A thorough obsession
vying for
a kiss.

My poetry is -

a candent ambition,
pregnant with desires
to excel.

A reckless rebel
against the vagaries
of established norms.

A chameleon-like camouflage
to put up
with this indifferent world.

A true mirror
to see the reflection
of my 'self'.

Life and Exploration

Years Spent

In the years gone by -
I have traversed the
length and breadth of
the realm of emotions,
through the depressing
trough of paroxysm,
to the heady
crest of ecstasy;
plied through the craggy
shorelines of loneliness,
berserk over a broken relationship,
wasting tears in solitude;
and reveled in the company of friends
sharing delectable raptures.

I have dictated my own terms
to this obstinate life,
unfettered by consequences,
and lived like a rebel
who belongs to none.

I have crumbled under duress
but got up afresh;
and now comes the time

when a butterfly will emerge
from its chrysalis,
shedding its cocoon,
flapping its wings,
billowing in the air,
ready to soar higher.

A Stranger

I am a stranger to myself,
unseen, unknown and unapprehended,
vast expanse of the realm
engulfing a cocoon of microcosm
deep within the phlegmatic soul;
entangled thoughts
lost in the labyrinth of a cerebral maze,
engendering burning regrets,
ensnared in my mind;
the pain, the anguish and the despair
lie nestled against my heart.

I dig deep into
my obscurity,
to douse
the scalding blaze of thoughts,
and move on
like a zombie,
celebrating my journey
towards the goal
not yet realized!

Span of These Seconds

I can feel
the pulse of this clock,
this elusive time-
slipping by,
moment by moment
from my grasp,
shrouding the present
into a distant past;
still, I clutch on
to these tiny morsels
of seconds
clinging onto my hands,
like a child
holding on to his Mama's fingers.

I can't let
this incessant
juggernaut of the tide,
quash my tempo;
I'll go on-
humming my melody,
a timbre of vital spark,
into the chronicle of
timeworn pages of history
extending from now to perpetuity.

That's Life

Life's little oddities
spring up-
often when uncalled for.

They catch me off guard,
throw me overboard
in the tumultuous water
of my 'rainy' past.

Memories leap forth-
crowding my 'mind space'.

As I reflect on
the difference between-
what was 'yesterday'
and what will be 'tomorrow',
I stumble upon
a grain of wisdom-
'the sharpest steel are those
that pass through hottest fire'.

I draw my lost strength
from the sinews of golden tomorrow-
even though I lay,
prostrate to the vagaries of 'life'.

This Is Not Me

I had it all planned out
in the crannies of my brain.
I have been thinking, you know.
But I wonder -
is dreaming still enough?

I had this idea of me.
But, where did I lose it?
This idea of me,
is she fading away
with each passing day?
I can't help feeling
I'm slowly inching towards giving up.
This is not me, I grew up with.

I can't help thinking,
I mull over the past -
brooding over might-have-it-could-have-been
if only I did let her know.

Instead, am left delirious -
ten degrees of separation,
nine shades of gray,
countless hours, so solitary
and endless smokes of cigarettes.

My Words

Here I fly again-
on the wings of my imagination,
away from the confines of
matter, space and time,
into the fourth dimension-
the immensity is contagious,
the landscape melts
onto the pallet of
turquoise horizon;
the solitude is transcendental,
the echo from deep within
resonates in my marrow
rendering me nimble;
moments and thoughts
converge on the
edge of existence-
juxtaposing
cacophony and bliss,
I need to test the
honesty of my selfishness.

I scribble ceaselessly,
as if my entrails
depend on these words for nutrition.

Notes of Musical Love

Have you ever heard a musical note?
A note that washes over your parched soul.
Engulfs you in its fold and immediately,
begins to nourish your inner glow.

Have you ever made a tender love?
Late into the early morning hours,
body rubbing against the delicate skin,
drawing out the nectar flowing with the rhythm.

Have you ever danced a carefree number?
Bereft of the sense of time or space,
pure energy and momentum blend into one,
feeding into your sense of happiness.

Have you ever painted a blank canvas?
Put colors of rainbow across your sky.
And followed the sun to a new day
with joy, brightness and sparkle on your feet.

Have you ever sung out loud?
The notes of your musical love,
out into the world that is waiting,
to embrace you in its warmth,
and letting you feel the lightness of being.

A Calling to Explore

Is there a one true calling
for everyone?
I know I want it all,
I want to do it all.

I want to run that marathon
and climb to the top of Kilimanjaro.
I want to ride my motorcycle across the
Pacific coast,
from San Francisco to San Diego.

I want to pack a punch
when I jab or hook.
Throw a deadly kick
when I kickbox or spar.
I want to be everything,
that I never was.
Yet I can be, me.

You Matter

You matter,
in your mind.
Believe me, you do.
The world is not enough,
for an oyster that's you.
You matter.

You are not even
a speck of dust,
in the history of time.
You will wither away.
You will soon fade.
This world will live to see another day.
Not even an iota of change,
in the timelessness of this Universe.
Or a Physicist may say,
maybe this is Multiverse.

You matter.
Just now,
just for today.
Tomorrow is unseen for you,
but the world will see yet another
day and night.
Like a rhythm,
with or without you.
You don't matter,
yet you do.

Books, Music and Coffee

Read a book today.
Let your mind be enamored,
with the beauty of a sentence.
And absorb the intellectual vitality
of being alive.

Listen to a song today.
Let your heart pulsate,
with the abundance of love
and dance with gay abandonment,
to the tune of your inner soul.

Savor a cup of coffee today.
Let your senses absorb the aroma
and mouth feel the wholeness
of an ecstasy,
that life brings every day!

Roots

You don't grow roots
by buying a house in a distant land.
Your roots are anchored
in your mind,
that harks back to
your home where you grew up.

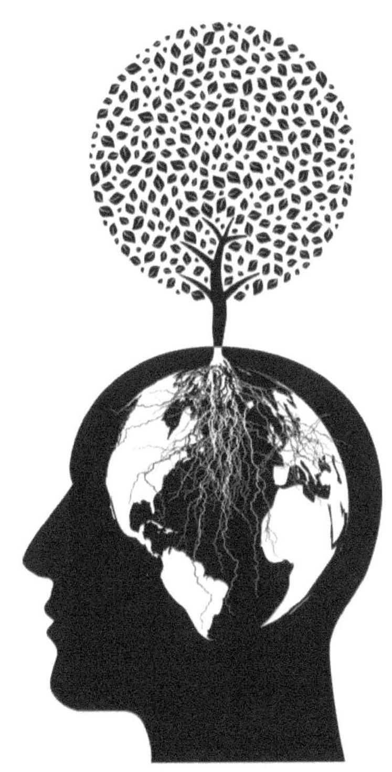

Simply Gifted

Your eyes dwell upon the
golden rays of the breaking dawn.
Sparkling a bright fire on the horizon
You are simply gifted to witness this day!

Your skin feels the nimble breeze,
caressing your face and hair,
lighting the warmth in your heart.
You are simply gifted to witness this play!

Your feet can take a hundred steps.
You can dance and waltz on your ankles,
brightening your spirit and energy.
You are simply gifted to witness this ray!

You smile and laugh cheerfully.
You exude happiness with whomever you meet,
nourishing the mind, heart and soul.
You are simply gifted to experience this joy!

You are alive.
You are energetic.
Live it in the moment,
this gift of time exists only for now.

The Light of My Life

The light of my life
reflected in your eyes,
illuminating my
joyous sprite.
This world is enough
I seek no heaven!

The light of my life
lit like a candle.
Burning bright,
nurturing my unbounded passion.
Your presence is enough.
I seek no other!

The light of my life.
Smoldering,
like a raging volcano
ready to burst forth in a fire.
Your eyes are the ocean.
I seek thee to drown myself!

A Muse

A vagabond mind.
Nothing anchors me like you.
Hold my face in your palms,
let me drink from the depth of your eyes!

A restless traveler,
searching for an oasis in the searing heat.
Weary, I lay by the wayside.
Resuscitate me with the moistness of your lips!

An intrepid fighter,
bruised and battered in the arena.
Shaken but still standing strong.
Revitalize me with the warmth of your arms!

Finding a Rhythm

That song on my mind
sparks a memory.
Distant but still fresh,
conjuring up the vision of a long-lost past.

That song on my mind
finds a rhythm of its own.
Playing like a symphony.
Lighting up the moments,
desires and emotions inter-mingling in a haze.

That song on my mind
strikes all the right chords.
Mixing the notes and tunes
to play the song of my life.

Staring into the Unknown

My book of life is being written.
A chapter has been closed
but this book is not over yet,
as I begin writing the next episode.

I might be down but not done yet.
Let a new tomorrow come,
let a new star shine on me.
I will write my story again.

The world feels just right, and
the days seem quietly bright.
I remember the song that fell out of me,
as I am staring into the unknown.

Twister

We are two lost souls
in the expansive sea of time,
floating amidst the vast emptiness,
drifting along on the swirls of waves.

Where would you go without me?
Where would I be without you?
Maybe in the same space-time continuum,
under the same, open turquoise sky.

The wave of time has got you hardened.
The rollicking ship has made me weary.
For I am a seafarer,
I will anchor the boat, no matter, the twister.

A Nudge of Memory

I begin to write my lines
to quench my longing for words.
It has been squatting on my throat
for who knows, how many years.

That word that we call 'nudge'.
It jumped out of my pen today.
As I sit lazily by the window,
watching the kids frolicking in the distance.

Their shrieks and laughter took me back
to my hometown in India.
I was a kid again,
playing in the dusty lanes on a humid evening.

I am startled by a nudge on my shoulder.
My pen makes my writing tense,
I decide to put a full stop,
there was this little me, smiling in the sunshine.

Across the Border

The blue sky still envelops
a thoughtful mind,
a child drowned in his books
in a faraway land in the rusty, hinterland of India.
Fond of his geography lessons,
opens the world map to locate the US of A.

Eyes wide with disbelief, at the
distance, the opulence, the opportunity
that lies across the oceans.
Lost in thought, he folds the map
to keep it away, safe as a prized possession.

The paper world map has now given way
to the feel of American soil,
under the feet of that grown-up child.
The sky still runs blue, enveloping
the countries across his map, over his still thoughtful
mind.
The color is the same, the feelings are the same,
thoughts are the same across the oceans.

Why was that hankering for that Promised Land?
The destination leads somewhere,

still nowhere.
Does the journey itself,
take a meaning larger than the destination?

The child is a grown man now.
After leaving the shores of the Indian Ocean,
he has been trying to go home,
for all his American life.

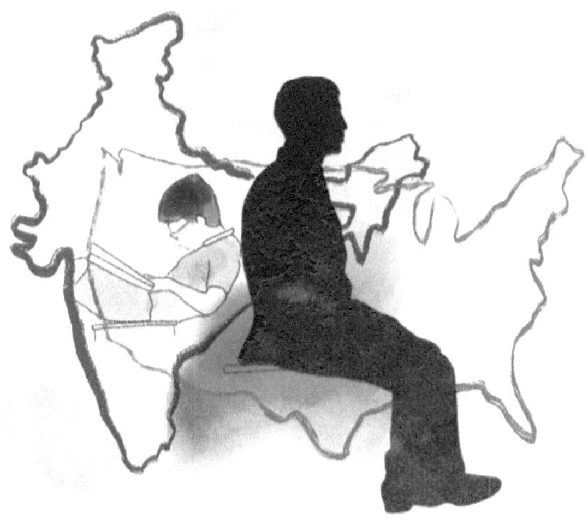

A Day

What will I do without you?
When the sun rises again
in the morning tomorrow,
I will be up on my feet,
drink my coffee, read my papers
and drive to work sharp at nine.
I will work my mind out
with a rivaled passion.
That was known only to you
or was it not?
I will talk and smile
and eloquently articulate how to win the business.
With a concerted effort,
that you saw in action
when I went after you.

When the dusk falls
and my mind is weary with the day's thought.
I will not rest still,
I will not sigh.
Where's my joy, my hope, my comfort?

I will live for
yet another tomorrow.
With warmth in my heart
that only you set it to glow!

Belongings

A book, my phone, a diary, a tablet
Seems I lie scattered all over my room.
I am breathing, I am alive,
and there is a part of me in my things around.

I live in my time, in my body
I desire, I lust, I talk, I laugh.
But I go to work too, day in and day out.
And come back to my things every night.

You see my things keep me anchored.
My mind is ablaze with searing thoughts,
my heart desires a peaceful voyage
and my soul burns with passion, a dozen.
I shift and turn as the changes in the season.
They say I am not a constant in this house,
anymore.

You see, with time,
I grew up, but my things did not.
I love them still but where is my heart?
My heart lay nestled in the frontiers
that might be just beyond my room here.

Overlooking the Golden Gate Bridge, SF

As you climb along the ramparts of Hawk hill,
the stunning panorama of Marine and San Francisco city
captures the imagination like your first love
holds afloat your heart, in a dreamy world.

The stunning red and orange twin towers,
rising gloriously from the blue pacific waters.
Grabs your attention as you peek through
its maze of sweeping cables and iron.

The majestic view has no other equals.
It may be controversial to say so,
but where can you come neck to neck
to witness this sensory experience of color and
sights?

I stare into the infinite distance of the ocean,
mists of haze and blue glow on the horizon.
I glance around the Golden Gate Bridge,
happy to soak in its art-deco and rugged charm.

Live Adventurously!

Have you climbed that mountain peak?
Have you run across that valley trail?
Have you cycled far and wide?
Or seen the world outside your narrow window yet?

Did you swim last evening out?
In the open sea, when deep blue water beckoned.
Or dived dangerously with mask and fins?
To see the world that lies beneath.

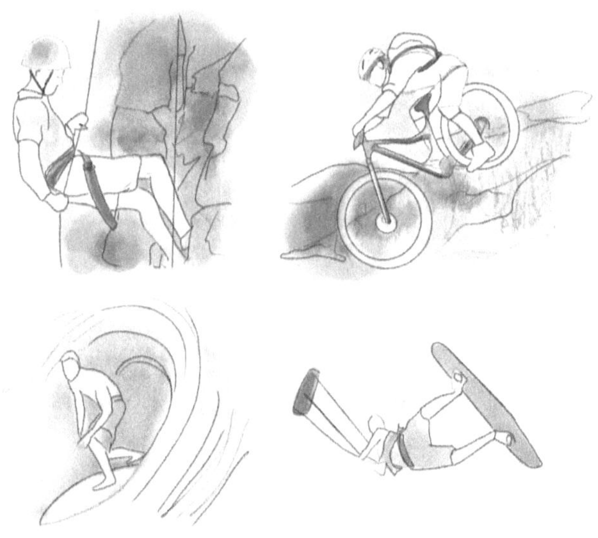

Have you piloted a hang glider in the air?
Or skydived from a high-up plane.
Don't you want to ski down the snowy slope?
Or skate in that ice rink, unhinged?

Why don't you ride that motorcycle,
And feel the freedom in your veins?
Why don't you answer that clarion call,
and hear that Summit calling, standing tall?
When you feel that you are done,
go outdoors, explore in the sun.
Lift your eyes unto that distant hill,
another challenge calls, another adventure awaits!

Freedom and Adventure

At Munnar: A Brush with Life

Miles of verdant greenery
gently, undulating lap of nature.
Fluffy, velvety clouds
breezing across,
the cool zephyr
rustling through,
the humming butterflies
wafting in thin air.
A herd of the Nilgiri tahr
galloping into the distant wood,
majestic waterfall in its vicinity
rushing through in all its grandeur.
The redolent ambiance,
the unbridled silence
(except the 'voices' of nature)
nestling in the wilderness-
lentissimo drizzle.
Soaking me wet;
I stand alone,
transfixed, mesmerized
experiencing
my inner self;
body in complete harmony
mind in immaculate peace,

spirit in blissful ecstasy;
rejuvenated.
I breathe again,
I can feel
the pulse of life
coursing through my veins.
After days of jejune existence,
I can sense again
the lightness of my being.

Fear or Fire

There is a tiny spark
smoldering just beneath my fear.
Raring its little head
whenever I want to leap.

Niggling fear or the raging fire.
Whom should I choose?
I choose fear,
feels my life begins to shrink.

I choose fire
I expand beyond my proportion.
Something inside of me
begins to take a shape.
That smoke from the smoldering fire
begins to clear,
as I leap,
beyond my courage.

It's My World!

I find myself too excited in my world,
The sunshine, the rolling hills, the green slopes.
I want to run across the meadows
and fly across the Sierras;
Dive deep into the abyss of the ocean.

Sometimes the world is not enough
to encompass the enormity of my dreams.
I want to throw punches like Ali
and be quick about it like Manny, the 'Pacman'.

Last winter I took up skiing,
and rolled with the slopes.
Steading my gait but falling nevertheless,
How can I tell you?
It still feels good to be a beginner.
Harking back to my childhood days.
Seeing this beautiful world with a fresh pair of eyes,
bereft of layers of dust with each passing day.

Let me hold my horses
of thoughts,
before they unleash another trail of dust
vanishing in the distance.
Sometimes I am too excited about this
garden-fresh world.

Miracle

Watching the sunrise
over the distant horizon.
The rolling hills,
in this verdant greenery.
This beautiful world is indeed
a grand miracle!

What a miracle it is!
Life emerged on this distant planet.
Greatest miracle
that consciousness emerged.
And what a miracle it is
that you and I live this moment.
You dug into my consciousness
and lit my soul on fire.
And I emerged a chrysalis, transformed.

You and I,
together, we are a miracle
that exist
in this enchanting world.

The Wind-Chaser: Driving through Wyoming

On this day
the sun was bright.
The sky was filled with shades of orange and blue,
the wilderness of Wyoming
was welcoming to my drive.

I was chasing the winds
solitary.
Untethered in the wild,
feeling the freedom
in my veins
to go, where I want to go.

The interplay of colors
on the horizon.
Cast a spell
on my mind.
I was racing my bike,
chasing the winds,
untethered in the wild.

Roaming the vastness
of my inner soul.
Seeking the wind in my hair,
fueling my fire within.
The journey outward was only a metaphor
to the unending horizon of my soul.

Overlooking Lake Chabot,
California

The white velvet
spread across the azure sky.
The gently undulating green slopes,
rolling hills and a deep blue oasis,
flowing through the turquoise landscape.

The gentle breeze swayed my long hair.
The feel of cool on my bare skin,
the panorama of striking beauty
soothing my tired eyes.

The climb across the overlook point
and the gentle exertion of the legs,
the calmness of the surroundings
seize my mind with a sense of peace.

It's in this nature that
the Zen of mind resides.
It's in the outdoors that
a sense of well-being pervades.

On Skydiving

Nothing to fear.
Nothing to hold back.
I took that leap
into the unknown!

What is to fear?
When down below
is the fluffy cloud
to lessen the blow.
Or further down
is the vast expanse of the ocean,
welcoming you to be like water,
not to resist, go with the flow
light and fluid, gentle and still.
Rest easy
in the lightness of
being alive.
What serenity,
joy and bliss!

I conquered my fear.

Mojo

I can write about a thousand things today.
So, I sit intently at my wooden desk, ready.
A few empty pages and reams of written pages
scribbled words staring back at me.

I dig deep in my heart.
My ethos, frothing at the seams,
ready to flow out of my pen.
What shall I write about today?

I soak my soul
in the depth of silence.
Playing with imaginary ideas,
firing my world with shimmering words,
squeezing some more of my newfound mojo.

Where Would You Ride To?

Down the open road
winding through the tall Eucalyptus.
It feels cooler in its shade
though it's blazing hot in May.

I come to a stop on my motorcycle
for a quick pause and recharge.
The rustling winds envelop my senses
And I cry out, this is freedom.

Freedom to ride in the meadows,
freedom to glide in the air.
Freedom so precious,
it clears the mind of ancient cobwebs.

I start my motorcycle again
a sleight of hand in the 'friction zone',
a slight roll of the throttle.
I am back on the road again.
I have tasted freedom.
I have experienced adventure.
I have lived the days of joy.

Freedom of an Open Road

Do you seek freedom?
the ultimate elixir of life.
Do you seek open roads?
the ultimate joy of a ride.

You are not alone, my friend.
But you got to pay the ransom.
You seek what's your destiny
but you got to chase your freedom.

I have been over the hills
and the rolling countryside,
I have seen a million faces
and made many friends.

On the trip, I felt joy and hope,
love and loss, melding into a
cauldron of emotions.
I let my hair and beard grow
And felt connected to my soul.
I opened my heart and mind
And felt sublime, at peace.

Freedom is the chosen destiny
get it with all your might.
The open road is a calling,
on your motorcycle, take a flight.

Guitar and Motorcycle

Music and Motorcycle,
both feed my soul.
They speak to my mind
when I am alone.

As I strum my guitar,
the plectrum pulls my heartstrings.
The energy, the vibe, the music
soak me into a Nirvana bliss.

As I rev my motorcycle,
the pulsating engine beats with my heart.
The clutch, the throttle, the gear
thrill me to the edge, beyond any fear.

On any Sunday,
play your guitar,
ride your motorcycle.
Level up a notch.

Create music, create memories
ride it relaxed, play it hard.
Meld these moments into your dream
wherever you go,
and when you arrive
you already had fun on the way.

The Red Fire

Have you felt the fire lately,
burning deep inside of you?
Raring to engulf, the enthralls,
of your heart, beating deep inside of you.

Rage, rage, against the time.
Race, race, against the mind.
Fly, fly, against the odds.
Run, run if you must.

Let the fire take its shape.
Let the embers manifest.
Outside your body and your mind.
Into a fiery, mean, racing machine.

Ride it if you only must.
Believe in your priceless freedom.
Race it if you can't stop
feeling the wind on your face

Ride it until the dawn breaks.
Ride it till the dusk settles.
A motorcycle is your spirit,
of the journey that lies ahead.

Pain and Loss

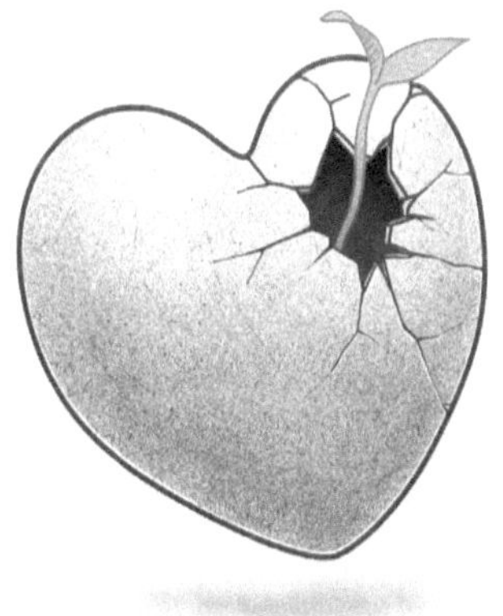

In a Moment

That moment now has
stripped itself
of all its meaning.

I'm insignificant.
But with each stroke
of my pen,
I aspire
to live again;
I have survived,
blood still coarse through
my thick veins.
Yes, I'm still alive.

Someone here
is so lonely.
There is no love,
no dim memories
bitter or sweet,
only blank verses
recoiling in a space.

I remain alone
in secrecy,
with my lost moments.

Rejoice!

I am free now-
released from the leashes
of thy haunting presence.
Free to be loved again,
free to be born again;
I (is it you?)
have ripped apart
the manacles of love,
the millstone around my neck.

Life has its taste,
I have drunk it to relish.
Thy exit from my life
I mourn not, but
I seek thee
in my silent grief.
Alas!
Indeed, I will rejoice.

Time for Self

In the helter-skelter of
tumultuous existence-
when life becomes a grind
and mind goes awry;
I aspire for
a moment to myself.

When the swirling cogitations
in the recesses of the brain,
hang like catacombs.
From the shriveled leaves
of my dry heart,
I crave for
a moment to myself.

When the vices of the world
smother my senses,
and numb silence prevailing around
shrieks like an orphan,
I long for
a moment to myself.

When the deep chasm 'within'
exposes my lacerated self-
pining for long-lost freedom,
I need
a moment to myself.

A Semblance of Sanity

The dusk crumples
into swelling darkness
outside my window.
The hour is tinged
with mercurial silence,
transmogrified into
the reverberation of jangle.
Moments were stolen from
pages of timeworn years,
a caravan of
mute words

flutters from my pen,
freezing-
the zillion mutinies within.
The palpitations
of the jaded heart
besieged impulsively by
the frisson of life,
seek a semblance of sanity
in the gathering monsoon
of torrid rain.

At the Crossroads

Beads of moments
plucked from the necklace of time,
adrift on the ocean
of my memory;
like a plectrum
pulls upon my heartstrings
rendering it vibrant,
sonorous of the times gone by.

Can I leave those
resplendent moments behind
and walk on?

Bright and Dark

Shadows lengthen-
as the sun
sneaks through the crevices
of the ragged door.

Silence wreaks havoc,
on the mind
gone awry,
as the music
blares in the vicinity.

I am forlorn,
in the midst of
a carousing crowd,
as I listen
rapt in attention
continuous thuds
from deep inside
of my conscience.

Consumed

The hunger is growing deep within me,
the thirst is scalding my parched soul,
desperately seeking nourishment
for my starving heart,
I am emaciated.
I gasp to breathe the melancholic air,
my heart pounds into the overweening silence;
the pieces of me I'll leave behind
scattered helter-skelter.
And the rest of me will
merge forever in the surging ocean;
I am all consumed
in my enormity.

Obsessed

Midnight.
The darkness slithers around
like a languid stream;
music, thoughts, moments...
arise in undulating waves,
crisscrossing the ebony stretch.

I stare in wonder,
at the slender, shining
orb of soft-glow light;
I'm enthralled
by its acute fervor,
I'm lost within
its comfortable warmth.
Its luminous presence
breaths perfection
into overweening silence,
kindling the fire within.

And in that moment,
I conceive a nugget.
It's the death of desires
when the heart begins to think.
So, my Orb,
escape me...
never..

Success and Achievement

Desires

My restless brain
churns out multitudinous desires,
burning with
candent ambition
to accomplish something tangible.

That creative energy
entrapped in my soul,
bound by the hectic drudgery
of my daily life;
seeks ephemeral vent
through the scribbling of my pen,
in the solitude of the night.

By the end of the day
still left with unfinished tasks,
I grapple with
the limits of my time.

Dreams

Irrepressible dreams
Shimmering in flambeau,
entangle my mind
like a cobweb,
holding on
with tenacity;
goading me
for the 'pursuit'.

Yet,
my perpetual tussle,
often rendered feckless;
leer at myself
posing a question-
Why do your dreams die young?

The Quest

Delving deep
into the deluge
of swirly cogitations,
I dig out
a catacomb of
lost memories,
dead wishes,
thwarted ambitions.
Like parasites
they cling to my soul,
nourishing themselves
with my marrow,
rendering a chasm
inside my corpus.

I close my eyes,
I seek my 'self'.
Like a Phoenix
rising from the embers
of burnt past,
my resilient 'self'
bounces back.
My asomatous body
floats in ethereal air;
rejuvenated,
I arise-
wide awaken
from my deep slumber.
In the quest of my true 'self'-
I pursue afresh
my future-
hopes, desires and ambitions.

Metamorphosis

Buried in the crypt of
forgotten time,
somewhere glows
a face of innocence.
I still hear that
careless laughter and idle bantering,
I relive those moments
when love and
fragile hopes
weaved magic in the heart.

I peel my thoughts
layer by layer,
dusting them with utmost care;
so much has changed
and so much remains the same-
In the ensuing period,
when did I grow up
to be a man?

On Jim Morrison

The name, Jim Morrison
the original rebel,
the poet and the rock star
Rolled into one.
The iconoclast.
Music drew its soul from him.
The Doors radiated the charm
that was him.

Yesterday I discovered
his lost diary
called 'Wilderness'.
I read his earlier verses
And lines scribbled in draft
I read intently
to find something
of the greatness that was him.

But all I could see.
It was plain
and simple.
Yet, it reflected his trials
and errors, the beginning of him.
That will become Jim Morrison.

If you don't do crap
to start with,
You can't do great things
when you grow up.

The Second Mountain

Driven, ambitious and passionate,
he had ascended the mountain peak.
Striving relentlessly, with a singular obsession
to climb, to strive and to reach the top.

The panorama was striking from his vantage point.
He felt like the conqueror who defeated all,
the wave of happiness swept like the breeze,
invincible he felt; superior he thought in his mind.

As the breeze calmed down, he felt an eerie silence.
Loneliness gnawed at his heart;
the emptiness echoed in his viscera.
'What was the point of it all?', he thought to himself.
His singular achievement meant so little to others.

Contemplating to himself, he narrowed his gaze
and saw the second mountain across the valley.
And lo and behold, it was teeming with people all
around.
He hurriedly climbed down and trekked across the
valley.

As he approached nearer, he saw people helping
each other
ascend the mountain.
Together they climbed and took the tumble
together,
negotiating the sharp bends on the way.
He soon realized it's not what you achieve
individually
but joy is in how you give away your energy
in the pursuit of affecting a positive change.

Joy is in helping, in giving, in supporting.
The Cause that deeply moves you
and making it larger than
just your individual self.

So, climb the first mountain, if you must.
To check your fitness on the way …
But remember, it's the second mountain,
where your impact will pave the others' way.

Love and Passion

Nature

I have seen
the panorama of blooming nature
radiant in your face.
Lost myself
in the ravines
of your fathomless eyes,
touched
the contours of
your silken cheek.
Drank the nectar
from the water-spring of

your crimson lips.
Sensed the intoxicating
whiff of your fragrance
permeating my sentience.

I am left delirious
amidst the enticing elements;
tell me -
where do I kiss thee
to complete the poetry
of your lyrical face?

The Silent Passion

Gusts of rhymeless breath-
resounds in the dark.
A deep moaning
wafts in the air-
the pain, the anguish, the craving
haunts the tumultuous heart.

Silence-
hangs in the air.
All-pervading and all-prevailing.
The mind-
reverberates
with feelings and emotions scattered
in the vast ocean of the distant past.

My life, dear-
is a cornucopia of your thoughts,
smoldering with ardent passion,
seeks permanent relief
at your heavenly bosom.

I Might Remember You

In solitude,
if I sit and think long enough
I might remember you.

I might remember
the way you smiled at me,
for that brief instant.
I might see
your radiant face,
I might feel the caress
of your soft tresses on my shoulder.

I may even reach out,
to feel your hand in mine.
Alas! In vain.

I ripped through the pages of the calendar
tearing asunder the days, months, years
that will never come.
When I will hear your voice again
if only for one last time.
My heart choking at the thought
that I may never see you again.

I clear my head
open my eyes.
One last puff on the cigarette,
and in the billowing smoke,
gone is the love
that I never felt for you.

Literate Love

My love reads you
line by line,
page after page,
as an open book.
Poring over every sentence,
reflecting on every paragraph,
it inexorably grapples with
the true significance
of every punctuation mark.

Yet I find-
the more I read,
the lesser I understand.
You remain an enigma,
a baffling conundrum,
a bewildering challenge
to my literate love.

I am lost
in the labyrinth of
your serpentine love.
I am searing
in the calescence of
your ardent desire.

A Rhapsody

Your memory comes forth
gushing like torrents of rain,
rocking the deep annals of my brain.
And there springs up a charming face
with an enigmatic smile on her lips
shining in the recesses of my heart.
Those brown eyes, radiant with life
sparkles on and on till eternity.
Those rosy lips full of vigor
outpours the warmth of your heart
beckoning me to your side.

Let your angelic hands
reach out in deep solace-
envelop me in an embrace
comfort the tingling of my nerves.

I lie down gasping for breath,
allured by your magical charm.
Longing for your arrival-
my rheumy eyes
still shedding dry tear-drops.

Abyss of Time

In the vast abyss of time
evolving into a swirling cloud
on the distant, forlorn horizon;
amidst the cacophony of
everyday crowded life,
snafu of somber existence.
You came as a tang
of fresh, redolent flowers
serenading into my life,

rejuvenating my whole being,
spawning young dreams
after years of jejune living.
It is destiny's own choice
that we have met-
after many a birth,
to bridge the chasm,
dividing eons
by our love till eternity.

I Am Free

Arms wide open,
outstretched
I'm falling.
Falling from this narrow ledge
of logic,
rationality,
to the unfathomed depths
of ludicrousness.
Absurd.
Reality. That's non-sense.

I tear myself open.
Blood drips down
from the gashes of unhealed wounds.

Light. Orb of fire.
I glare at the sun.
Dissolve into the ethereal air,
hazy clouds clear
from the tentacles of mind.

I emerge out.
Naked. Reborn.
Did I love you?
The voice echoes
between my ears,
I strain to hear an answer.

At last,
there is a sense in this madness.
I am free.

Intervening Silence

It has been ages-
since we parted.
Nothing remains
but the intervening silence;
a vague sensation,
an ineffable feeling
of vast timelessness.

The mundane life
takes its course.
Only time flows by-
between you and me,
giving some meaning
to this inane love.

Jabberwocky

Lilting tunes,
soothing breeze,
bewitching eyes,
candle-light,
frozen moment,
whiff of fragrance,
sinning silence,
throbbing heart,
shreds of hope,
river of dreams,
the flow of thoughts,
unhinged desires,
throes of passion,
ruminating soul,
drama within,
angst & sigh!

A Magical Moment

The ecumenical silence
enveloping the ambience
creates music in my ears.
The charisma of your presence
heals my lacerated heart,
pining for your attention.
Those fleeting seconds
weave magic in the air
lingering at my heartstrings
until you are long gone.

The moment in your company
is an elixir for my jejune life,
it's sweet sensations
transcend the worldly pleasures.

Null and Void

My elixir,
I accept
I am no Adonis.
But my love,
take hold of me;
render me plenitude,
as I am
without you
null and void.

Psychedelic Love

Vivid golden light
plays upon the azure sky,
the zenith above
glows in harlequin resplendence.
The kaleidoscopic scintillation
paints the ambience,
in surreal charm;
distance glows and shimmers,
basked in luminous effulgence;
naked silence
reins inside the glass window-pane;
light and colors spill
over shuddering walls.

In quivering delight,
two celestial bodies
unite in conjugal bliss.

Solace

I have been rambling
across the frontiers
of time and space
since eons;
like a vagabond
traversing the path,
on the welkin and beyond
untied, untrammeled;
seeking refuge
in my anomie;
looking for -
sentience in its perpetuity.

Support me with
thy enchanting presence.
Tender me love,
kiss me-
before I breathe again.

Vacuum

I can hear today
the melody of silence,
a low, poignant tune
of emptiness in this darkness.
A deep gash in my heart-
dim shadows of time
crawling at the edge of memory.
Is it you?
An unrevealed image of beauty,
or icon of an enigma.

Numb darkness slithers around,
enshrouding the soreness of my soul.
Let there be light-
my memories need to see itself
clearly in the mirror,
an image of your beauty,
an image of my own life.

I quiver
at the touch of your soft skin,
the comfort of your fingers
against my burning cheek;
sheathed in utter loss.

I hold you tight against my heart.
When the mist clears
from my languid eyes,
you are no longer there
and I am left
nursing the vacuum in my heart.

Your Music

Your music makes love
to my dry soul,
that sponges off
all the moisture from your melody.
And blooms like a rainbow,
anchoring on a pillar of hope
towards the near horizon.

Your music creates a desire
in my parched body
to soak in your embrace.
And live in the moment,
filling my heart with a hope
that colors my world, bright.

Your music is a sensation
a dream, a trance
and a meditation
for my tired mind,
to rest on your desires.

Come, Light My Fire!

I lie scattered
across my books,
my guitar, my bike, my gears.
Raptured in my thoughts
ensnared in my worldly trope.

I get up and run
far across the park
across the hiking trails.
Climbing atop the mountain dome,
running to set myself free.

Do you want to come?
Enter my world.
Re-order my belongings,
calm my parched soul.
Come, light my fire!

The Moon & the Sun

I want you
like the moon wants the sun.
I am in a dark place,
bereft of any semblance of light
shining on my heart,
Without you.

Your charm
lights my cloudy days,
lifts the fog up
and I can see miles ahead.

Shine your eyes on me
feed me that ray of hope.
Like a butterfly hovering on the sunflower
in the gently breaking dawn,
feed me the nectar that I so desire.

Literature

She was intense
just like me.
Her mind was nectar,
drawing me in.
Her eyes had a charm,
unknown to me
Her lips had a life,
taming my wild.
Her face was serene,
pulling me in.
Her body was an aphrodisiac,
resist, I couldn't.

I can love her
or lose her.
Maybe suffer in the process.
Until I found a third way
and turned her into
my lines.
And I wanted to call her,
Literature.

Epilogue

Create!

Create a few lines on a page
it could be the birth of poetry.

Create poetry.
Create a book.
Create a piece of art.
Create a short film.
Create a musical piece.
Create a community.
Create a business.
Create a life.
To touch other lives!

"I am large, I contain multitudes'

— *Song of Myself* by Walt Whitman